To:

GW00494619

BELIEVE

Written and compiled by
Barbara Paulding

PETER PAUPER PRESS, INC.
White Plains, New York

For Margit Ofstie Paulding,
whose belief in all her children
has helped us also believe.

Designed by La Shae V. Ortiz

Copyright © 2014
Peter Pauper Press, Inc.
202 Mamaroneck Avenue
White Plains, NY 10601
All rights reserved
ISBN 978-1-4413-1471-0
Printed in China
7 6 5 4 3 2 1

Visit us at www.peterpauper.com

dream **DARE**
SHOOT FOR THE MOON
DISCOVER
leap soar smile
BELIEVE
CREATE SING
BE FEARLESS YOUR
BLOSSOM SONG
BE AMAZING

INTRODUCTION

You can, you should, and if you're brave enough to start, you will.

—Stephen King

Believing isn't about closing your eyes and wishing really hard. It's about clearing away everything untrue to let the sun rise on your gift, your right work, your perfect imperfection. As we wade through possibilities in this chaotic and messy world, we sometimes forget the magic of knowing that—no matter the

circumstances—we still have the twin seeds of potential and passion inside. Now is the time to realize that we are exactly where we need to be to clear the way, to say a hearty "yes," to invent with audacious belief the life that lights us up. And to share that light with the world. Believe in yourself!

AS **SOON** AS YOU **TRUST** YOURSELF, YOU *will know* HOW TO LIVE.

—*Johann Wolfgang von Goethe*

YOU ARE WHAT YOU *believe* YOURSELF TO BE.

—Paulo Coelho

THE UNIVERSE
IS CHANGE; OUR
LIFE IS WHAT OUR
thoughts MAKE IT.

—Marcus Aurelius

MAGIC IS
BELIEVING IN
yourself. IF YOU
CAN DO THAT,
YOU CAN MAKE
ANYTHING
HAPPEN.

—*Johann Wolfgang
von Goethe*

WHETHER YOU
BELIEVE YOU CAN
DO A *thing* OR NOT,
YOU'RE RIGHT.

—*Henry Ford*

AS FOR
THE *future,*
YOUR TASK IS NOT
TO FORESEE IT,
BUT TO
ENABLE IT.

—*Antoine de Saint-Exupéry*

YOUR *thoughts*
ARE THE
ARCHITECTS OF
YOUR *destiny*.

—David O. McKay

I BELIEVE THAT
EVERYTHING HAPPENS
FOR A REASON.
PEOPLE **CHANGE**
SO THAT YOU CAN
LEARN TO LET GO . . .
AND SOMETIMES GOOD
THINGS FALL APART
SO *better* THINGS CAN
FALL TOGETHER.

—*Marilyn Monroe*

ALL GREAT
DEEDS AND
ALL GREAT
thoughts HAVE A
RIDICULOUS
BEGINNING.

—*Albert Camus*

WHAT LIES *behind* US
AND WHAT LIES
BEFORE US ARE
TINY MATTERS
compared TO WHAT
LIES WITHIN US.

—*Ralph Waldo Emerson*

NOT KNOWING WHEN THE DAWN WILL COME, I OPEN EVERY DOOR.

—Emily Dickinson

NOTHING CAN DIM
THE *light* WHICH SHINES
FROM WITHIN.

—*Maya Angelou*

TO ACCOMPLISH GREAT THINGS,
WE MUST NOT ONLY ACT,
BUT ALSO DREAM;
NOT ONLY PLAN,
BUT ALSO *believe*.

—*Anatole France*

I HOPE YOU WILL GO
OUT AND LET *stories*
HAPPEN TO YOU, AND
THAT YOU WILL **WORK**
THEM, ***water*** THEM
WITH YOUR BLOOD
AND TEARS AND YOUR
laughter TILL THEY
BLOOM, TILL YOU
YOURSELF BURST
INTO BLOOM.

—*Clarissa Pinkola Estés*

IT'S KIND OF FUN TO DO THE *impossible.*

—*Walt Disney*

YOU ARE A CHILD OF
THE **UNIVERSE,**
NO LESS THAN THE
TREES AND THE STARS;
YOU HAVE A RIGHT TO
BE HERE.

—*Max Ehrmann,*
DESIDERATA

SOME THINGS

HAVE TO BE

believed TO

BE SEEN.

—Ralph Hodgson

WHATEVER

YOU CAN DO,

OR *dream* YOU CAN DO,

BEGIN IT.

Boldness HAS GENIUS,

POWER, AND

MAGIC IN IT.

—*Author unknown*

THERE IS NO GREATER
GIFT YOU CAN GIVE OR
RECEIVE THAN TO
honor your calling.
IT IS WHY YOU WERE BORN
AND HOW YOU BECOME
MOST TRULY *alive.*

—*Oprah Winfrey*

LIFE LOVES TO
BE TAKEN BY THE
LAPEL AND TOLD,
"I'M WITH YOU
KID. *Let's go.*"

—*Maya Angelou*

WHEN YOU
WANT SOMETHING,
ALL THE UNIVERSE
CONSPIRES IN
helping YOU TO
ACHIEVE IT.

—Paulo Coelho

SOUND
THE NOTE THAT
calls YOUR SOUL
TO YOU.

—*Sanaya Roman*

LIFE IS EITHER A *daring* ADVENTURE OR NOTHING AT ALL.

—*Helen Keller*

SOMETIMES
I'VE *believed* AS
MANY AS SIX
IMPOSSIBLE
things BEFORE
BREAKFAST.

—*Lewis Carroll,*
THROUGH THE
LOOKING-GLASS

MOST OF ALL ON YOUR
JOURNEY,
BE PATIENT AND *believe*
in yourself. YOU WILL
MEET THE PEOPLE
YOU'RE SUPPOSED TO
MEET . . . AND
EXPERIENCE
WHAT YOU ARE MEANT
TO EXPERIENCE.

—*Eric Saperston*

FAITH IS TAKING THE FIRST *step* EVEN WHEN YOU DON'T SEE THE WHOLE STAIRCASE.

—Martin Luther King, Jr.

THE BIG
QUESTION IS
WHETHER YOU
ARE GOING TO
BE ABLE TO **SAY A**
HEARTY *yes*
TO YOUR
ADVENTURE.

—*Joseph Campbell*

Be fearless.
HAVE THE COURAGE
TO TAKE **RISKS**. GO
WHERE THERE ARE NO
GUARANTEES.
GET OUT OF YOUR
COMFORT ZONE, EVEN
IF IT MEANS BEING
uncomfortable.

—*Katie Couric*

Believe YOU
CAN AND YOU'RE
HALFWAY
THERE.

—*Theodore Roosevelt*

IF ONE
ADVANCES
CONFIDENTLY IN THE
DIRECTION OF HIS
DREAMS, AND
ENDEAVORS TO *live the*
life which he has
imagined, HE WILL MEET
WITH A *success*
UNEXPECTED IN
COMMON HOURS.

—*Henry David Thoreau*

THOSE WHO
DON'T BELIEVE
IN *magic*
WILL NEVER
FIND IT.

—*Roald Dahl*

NO **PERSON** HAS THE RIGHT TO *rain* ON YOUR DREAMS.

—*Marian Wright Edelman*

IF YOU WANT TO

CONQUER
FEAR,

DO NOT SIT HOME AND

THINK ABOUT IT.

Go out and get busy.

—Dale Carnegie

The most courageous act IS STILL TO THINK FOR YOURSELF. *Aloud.*

—*Coco Chanel*

IT IS **NEVER**
too late to be
WHAT YOU
MIGHT HAVE
BEEN.

—*George Eliot*

LET YOURSELF BE
SILENTLY DRAWN BY
THE STRANGE PULL
OF WHAT YOU
REALLY LOVE.
IT WILL NOT LEAD
YOU ASTRAY.

—*Rumi*

LIFE *shrinks* OR
EXPANDS IN
PROPORTION TO
ONE'S *courage*.

—Anaïs Nin

MAKE THE *world*
BEFORE YOU A BETTER ONE
BY GOING INTO IT WITH
ALL **BOLDNESS**. YOU
ARE UP TO IT AND YOU ARE
FIT FOR IT; YOU **DESERVE**
IT AND IF YOU MAKE YOUR
OWN *best* CONTRIBUTION,
THE WORLD BEFORE YOU
WILL BECOME A BIT MORE
DESERVING OF YOU.

—Seamus Heaney

TO SEE THINGS
IN THE SEED,
THAT IS GENIUS.

—Lao-Tzu

PERHAPS I AM
STRONGER THAN
I THINK.

—Thomas Merton

Believe in yourself!
HAVE FAITH IN YOUR
ABILITIES! WITHOUT
A **HUMBLE** BUT
REASONABLE CONFIDENCE
IN YOUR OWN *powers*
YOU CANNOT BE
SUCCESSFUL
OR HAPPY.

—*Norman Vincent Peale*

WHEREVER
YOU GO, GO WITH
ALL YOUR *heart*.

—Confucius

Stuff YOUR EYES WITH
WONDER . . . LIVE
AS IF YOU'D DROP DEAD
IN TEN SECONDS.
See the world.
IT'S MORE
FANTASTIC THAN ANY
DREAM . . .

—*Ray Bradbury,*
FAHRENHEIT 451

WE DO NOT NEED MAGIC
TO **CHANGE THE
WORLD**, WE CARRY
ALL THE *power* WE NEED
INSIDE OURSELVES
ALREADY: WE HAVE
THE POWER TO
IMAGINE BETTER.

—*J. K. Rowling*

Believe ANYTHING
IS POSSIBLE
AND THEN WORK LIKE
HELL TO MAKE IT
HAPPEN.

—Julianna Margulies

YOUR DREAMS,

WHAT YOU HOPE FOR
AND ALL THAT, IT'S NOT
separate FROM YOUR
LIFE. IT GROWS RIGHT
UP OUT OF IT.

—Barbara Kingsolver

DON'T LIVE DOWN
TO EXPECTATIONS.
GO OUT THERE AND
DO SOMETHING
REMARKABLE.

—Wendy Wasserstein

WE ARE ALL PART
OF CREATION,
ALL KINGS, ALL POETS,
ALL MUSICIANS; WE
HAVE ONLY TO OPEN UP,
TO *discover* WHAT IS
ALREADY THERE.

—*Henry Miller*

FROM TIME TO TIME YOU
MAY STUMBLE. . . . BUT
I KNOW THIS, IF YOU'RE
WILLING TO BE GUIDED
BY THAT *still small voice*
THAT IS THE G.P.S. WITHIN
YOURSELF . . . YOU WILL BE
happy, YOU WILL BE
SUCCESSFUL, AND
YOU WILL MAKE
A DIFFERENCE IN
THE WORLD.

—*Oprah Winfrey*

THE **LIGHT** OF
starry dreams CAN
ONLY BE SEEN ONCE
WE ESCAPE THE
BLINDING CITIES
OF DISBELIEF.

—*Shawn Purvis*

PROMISE ME
YOU'LL *always*
REMEMBER:
YOU'RE **BRAVER**
THAN YOU BELIEVE, AND
STRONGER THAN YOU
SEEM, AND **SMARTER**
THAN YOU THINK.

—*Christopher Robin,*
FROM A. A. MILNE'S
WINNIE THE POOH

YOUR **PLAYING**
small DOES NOT SERVE
THE WORLD. THERE IS
NOTHING ENLIGHTENED
ABOUT *shrinking* SO
THAT OTHER PEOPLE
WON'T FEEL INSECURE
AROUND YOU. WE ARE ALL
MEANT TO **SHINE**,
as children do.

—*Marianne Williamson*

All THE POSSIBILITIES OF YOUR *human* DESTINY ARE ASLEEP IN YOUR SOUL. YOU ARE HERE TO REALIZE AND HONOR THESE POSSIBILITIES.

—*John O'Donohue*

IT IS NOT
BECAUSE THINGS
ARE *difficult*
THAT WE DO NOT
DARE, IT IS
BECAUSE WE DO
NOT DARE THAT
THEY ARE
DIFFICULT.

—*Seneca*

OUR DUTY,

AS MEN AND WOMEN,

IS TO *proceed* AS IF
LIMITS TO OUR
ABILITY DID NOT EXIST.
WE ARE **collaborators**
IN CREATION.

—*Pierre Teilhard de Chardin*

YOU ARE NEVER
GIVEN A *wish*
WITHOUT ALSO
BEING GIVEN THE
power TO MAKE
IT COME TRUE.
YOU MAY HAVE TO
WORK FOR IT,
HOWEVER.

—*Richard Bach*

HAVE THE *courage*
TO FOLLOW YOUR HEART
AND INTUITION. THEY
SOMEHOW ALREADY KNOW
WHAT YOU *truly* WANT TO
BECOME. EVERYTHING
ELSE IS SECONDARY.

—*Steve Jobs*

THE FUTURE
STARTS *today*,
NOT TOMORROW.

—JOHN PAUL II

ONE DOESN'T

discover NEW

LANDS WITHOUT

CONSENTING TO

LOSE SIGHT,

FOR A VERY

LONG TIME, OF

THE SHORE.

—André Gide

WALK WITH THE DREAMERS,

THE BELIEVERS . . .
SUCCESSFUL PEOPLE WITH
THEIR HEADS IN THE *clouds*
AND THEIR FEET ON THE
GROUND. LET THEIR SPIRIT
ignite a fire WITHIN YOU
TO LEAVE THIS WORLD
BETTER THAN WHEN
YOU FOUND IT.

—*Wilferd Peterson*

I BELIEVE IN BEING **STRONG** WHEN
EVERYTHING SEEMS TO
BE GOING WRONG. . . .
I BELIEVE THAT
tomorrow IS
ANOTHER DAY, AND
I BELIEVE IN
MIRACLES.

—*Audrey Hepburn*

TEND TO YOUR DREAM
AND SING YOUR SONG.
THAT SONG IS THERE TO
educate YOU, IT'S THERE
TO HOLD YOUR HAND,
ENTERTAIN YOU, AND
nourish YOU IN THE BEST
AND WORST OF TIMES.

—*Wynton Marsalis*

IF WE ALL DID
THE THINGS WE
ARE *capable* OF
DOING, WE WOULD
LITERALLY
ASTOUND
OURSELVES.

—Thomas Edison

NOTHING **SPLENDID** HAS EVER BEEN *achieved* EXCEPT BY THOSE WHO *dared* BELIEVE THAT SOMETHING INSIDE THEMSELVES WAS **SUPERIOR** TO CIRCUMSTANCE.

—*Bruce Barton*

THROW YOUR DREAMS INTO SPACE LIKE A *kite*,
AND YOU DO NOT KNOW
WHAT IT WILL BRING BACK,
A NEW LIFE,
A NEW FRIEND, A NEW
LOVE, OR A NEW COUNTRY.

—*Anaïs Nin*

ALL THE REALLY *exciting* THINGS POSSIBLE DURING THE COURSE OF A LIFETIME REQUIRE A LITTLE MORE *courage* THAN WE CURRENTLY HAVE. A DEEP BREATH AND A LEAP.

—*John Patrick Shanley*

DON'T BE
AFRAID TO BE
amazing.

—Andy Offutt Irwin

Images used under licen
Pages 14, 30, 46, 54, 62,
Page 22 © tolchik, 201
Front Endpapers, Pag